PANTY CLAUS

MAHOGANY B. PRESTON

D1714538

THE
MBP

ISBN: 978-1-959253-28-0

First printing, 2024 by Mahogany B. Preston

<u>Trigger Warnings</u>
- Heavy Steam
- Taboo Content
- Forced Proximity
- Praise
- Promiscuousness

To Those Of Us That Can Keep A Secret
Yours Are Safe With Me
MBP

It's all fun and games 'til Santa checks the naughty list.

— UNKNOWN

CHAPTER 1

BELISE

"Look out!" Cash drapes one hand across my chest and points the other at a statuesque deer leaping across the road.

The tires shriek like cats clawing at each other as the car swerves off the road into a pile of snow. When we stop screaming and catch our breath, we look at each other.

"Is everyone alright?" I ask, looking down at Cash's deep tan hand pressed firmly over my breasts. "I'm good now." I smile at her.

She smiles back with her almond eyes, always *smizing*. "That's a natural reaction. I wasn't feeling you up."

"Girl, please. Everyone wants to feel these babies." I shimmy until my boobs bounce.

Cash fans me off. "You alright back there?" she asks Penny, sitting in shock with her mouth wide open and red face nearly burnt from the jolt of the car.

She nods. "Just freaked out a little. Was that a moose?"

"A buck, I think." Cash frowns, looking back at her. "Do you know how big an actual moose is?"

Penny's brow raises. "No. But the antlers on whatever that was were huge."

"A moose is probably three times the size of what we missed. *Waaaay* bigger than that thing," I add. "Good eye, Cash."

"Good driving." She sways her racy wine hair from her face. "I probably would have hit it with my heavy foot."

"It was dangerous of me to hit the brakes like that in these conditions. I should have let it hit us."

"Don't say that." Penny taps my shoulder. "We could be in worse shape. Now start the car up. We have my sendoff to get to."

I press the button, and it doesn't crank. I pump the brakes twice, press the button again, and sit back.

"This is why I miss cars with a key and ignition." I turn to Cash. "Don't you dare sing that damn song."

She hums, *"Let me stick,"* from behind curved pressed lips.

"This isn't a laughing matter." Penny hugs herself. "It's already getting cold in the car. Stop playing, Belise, and crank this bitch up."

"I'm not playing. It won't start, and I don't want to flood the engine."

"I'm calling roadside." Penny dials on her phone.

Cash suggests, "Call one of the other girls. The resort is forty minutes away. One of them can come get us."

The background noise of Cali's latest banger has the rest of the bridal party going wild when Naz answers.

"Naz! We have an issue with our car! We need you to come get us! I'm sending you the drop!"

"I've already had too many. I'll send Cece. She's been sulking and boring as fuck since we got here. She won't mind. See y'all in a bit."

An hour later, we're still on the side of the road. Cece isn't answering her phone, and the roadside truck has yet to arrive. Cash and Penny are huddled together in the backseat below a crocheted blanket, and the panic on their faces sends me into protect-the-pack mode.

"Hear me out. We have about an hour left of daylight. Not one car has passed us, and the temps will continue to drop."

Penny sighs. "I don't like where this is headed."

I squeeze the steering wheel. "I said hear me out. I'm assuming that entrance back there leads to the big house we saw when we came around that curve. I'm gonna take the pistol and leave you two with the stun gun while I walk up there to find someone to help us."

Cash frowns. "By yourself?"

"Best to do it while we have sunlight and our phones are working. So, sit tight, and I'll call when I get up there."

CHAPTER 2

BELISE

I'm stuffed like Ralphie's little brother on the top half of my body, but no matter how warm I am, the chill cutting my nose and cheeks between the scarf wrapped in layers around my neck makes my body still feel cold.

I listen out for snapping tree branches and grunts of wild animals with my finger on the trigger of the pistol in my front coat pocket. I'm the bravest in the car, though I'm afraid of the wilderness. Even still, I'd rather risk finding help while the sun is out instead of freezing to death in the car when help could be near.

The sloshing sound of my boots trekking through the snow becomes ASMR along the way. I begin counting my steps when light snowflakes fall on the paved, snow-dusted road, and the house appears in the distance.

I make it to the gate of the estate. The black iron protecting the fortress isn't visible from the street, but it's unlocked. I make my way inside with my trigger finger ready to shoot just in case a vicious guard dog attacks me.

"Can I help you?" asks a man from the side of the house.

He's layered in workman's clothing, a wool cap with the eyes and mouth cut out, brown leather gloves, and steel boots. I stop in my tracks and clinch the gun in my pocket as the six-foot-two figure approaches.

"Actually, yes. My friends and I were run off the main road by a deer, and now our car won't start. I'm hoping someone can help us get it started or take a look at it."

He lifts the cap. "I have a few things I need to finish up out here, but I can take a look at it for you. Let me grab the lady of the house. Maybe you can sit with her while I pull the truck around."

"Thanks," I say, rocking myself back and forth to keep warm.

The snow picks up with a gust of wind that nearly tips me over. A young, light-brown woman about my age steps outside and waves at me to come forward. I hide my confusion about the man calling her *lady of the house* by the time I'm standing in front of her.

"Hi, I'm Belise." I shake her hand with the one not gripping the gun.

"Nice to meet you. Bellamy Kingsburd. Please come in. You must be freezing. Brent told me a woman was out here alone, and I hurried up to the main house immediately."

"Sorry for the intrusion."

"Oh, it's no problem at all. I was just putting away decorations and slicing a cake that's about to go to waste thanks to the storm ruining the first wedding I've booked since August."

"I only just arrived, but this place is beautiful from what I can see. And full of Christmas trees. I love that. I'd book my wedding here if I were to get married."

"Thank you. It's hard to compete with other venues closer to the city. Especially at Christmas. Thank God for deposits. Am I right?"

"Right."

"Come sit in the den. My best friend and a *very* hands-on bride are in there making sure the champagne doesn't go to waste."

I follow her thin frame down the wooden hallway wide enough to fit a double-wide trailer inside. Her curly hair hangs down her back and is stiff as she walks. Deer game heads and family portraits decorate a dim hall where the dwindling sunlight creeping inside makes it look like she's leading me into heaven.

The heat from the fireplace thawing me out feels like I have just crossed the pearly gates. I exhale for the first time since the long trek in the snow, take my hand off the trigger, and slip on the safety before taking off my coat.

"Girls. This is Belise."

"Belise, this is my best friend, Sam, and this is my client Claire."

"Cheers." Claire raises her glass. "I'm the bride... was a bride." She sips from the bottle. "This storm is a sign."

I remove my gloves. "Nice to meet you both."

"Likewise." Sam's glare is frosty behind her green eyes.

Her short, tapered haircut is reminiscent of the eldest Braxton. I almost tell her she looks like her when she ignores me and takes Claire by the hand.

"And you *are* a bride. You signed the license weeks ago. This was just the party."

"I guess."

I interrupt. "If you don't mind me asking...did the forecast change or something?"

Sam smacks her pink-coated lips. "Those meteorologists never know what they're talking about."

Claire's pale hand lifts her phone to my face. "I know more about what's headed this way using a weather app."

I stare at the word *blizzard* written in bold caps on her screen. She withdraws her cell and finishes off the bottle.

"They said two to three inches. Shit. The winds picked up when I made it to your house. I need to get back to my friends."

"Brent! We can finish out back later. Tow Belise's car up here." Bellamy squeezes my shoulder. "You and your friends can stay here until the storm passes."

"Thanks, but we probably only need a jump. We called for roadside and sent for a friend to come pick us up." I look at the time on my phone. "She and my other friends are most likely waiting for me to come back, I'm sure."

Claire warns me, "If your friend is coming from the resorts in Martis Valley Trail or Truckee, she probably turned around. The storm hit there thirty minutes ago. It's where my in-laws are staying."

"That's where we're headed. One last hurrah for my

friend who's getting married on New Year's." I sigh. "If you'll excuse me."

"Let me grab you a coffee." Bellamy runs off.

I step into the hallway and call Naz. No answer. Next, I dial Cece. She answers in a panic.

"Where are you?"

"At a house off the main road. Are you with Cash and Pen?"

"No, I had to turn around and come back to the cabin. The police have the roads blocked. They say it isn't safe to travel. The roads are icing, and the storm is coming in faster."

"Well, I'm glad you're safe. That's one less thing to worry about. Look, you guys go ahead and do every-thing we planned. We'll be stranded at this nice woman's house during the blizzard. I'm pinging our location so you know where we are."

"Got it. Sorry if I let you down, Lise."

"Don't be. Everything's fine. See you guys soon." I hang up the call.

"You mind riding back down there with me so your friends know I'm there to help?" A deep voice startles me.

I hold my chest. "Umph. I didn't hear you walk up."

Brent's brown eyes glisten.

"Sure," I stammer. "Yeah."

"Follow me."

I steal glances at his tight jeans wrinkling when his leg lifts to press on the gas then the brakes. From where I sit, his brown eyes captivate me in the rearview win-dow. His profile is sexy against the backdrop of white-covered mounds, and the scruff on his chin secretly requests me to run my fingernails through the stubble.

I fantasize what his rough hands feel like brushing against my skin, and just as I imagine them tracing my thirsty lips, the daydream comes to an abrupt halt.

"Good thing I cleared the roads yesterday," he says. "That pile of snow stopped you ladies from falling into that ditch."

"Thank you. For that and for this."

"Happy to help." He smiles at me. "I'll keep the truck running so you ladies can stay warm."

"I appreciate that."

I hop out and tell the girls what's going on. Penny is livid she's going to miss her bachelorette party, but I assure her there's enough booze at this house to more than make up for it.

"This is Brent, by the way."

He nods. "How y'all doing?"

"Cold." Penny shivers, stuffing her long tight coils in her cap.

Brent knocks on the hood. "Pop it for me."

I mumble, "I got no problem doing that."

Penny hops on her feet. "Who is this man?"

"I'm tryna find out. Go. Get in the truck. He kept it running so you two could get warm." I lean into her and whisper, "And get in the back."

Penny chortles and shares my message with Cash.

"No fair," says Cash, winking at me. "That man is hot, and I could use some heating up. Let's give him his first threesome," she whispers in my ear.

I mumble, "A handsy man like that." I sneak a peek at him. "Doubt it'd be his first time."

The girls stare at me inching closer to Brent hooking up jumper cables.

"Try to crank it when I tell you. Okay?"

I climb behind the wheel and wait for his signal. The engine refuses to turn. He unhooks the cable. I grab my purse and hop out.

"Good thing is, it's not your battery. Impact often times kills the fuel pump. I can reset the crash sensor in a day. Maybe two. Which pans out since you'll be stuck here for that long anyhow."

"Two days?"

"The main roads don't get salted until the snow stops. You ladies are stuck here."

I scoff. "I can pay you—for helping us."

He looks up at me and mumbles something as he winds the cables into a tight coil, holding me with a steely gaze that makes the muscle between my legs spasm.

"What was that?"

"I'm gonna pull your car back up to the house. Get back in the truck and warm yourself up. I've got everything under control out here."

"Yes, sir."

The girls and I watch Brent uncoil the tow line. When he jumps back in the truck to maneuver it in front of the car, we silence our gossip like men do when a woman enters a barbershop.

"Thank you for saving us." Cash makes a play at him.

I roll my eyes at her as she scrunches her nose at me.

"It's no problem." Brent blushes.

We laugh when he hops back out to hook up the

car. As it lifts from the ground, we fall silent when the headlights shine on the print of his glory resting on his thigh.

"I might have to fight you for this one," says Cash.

"I brought Vaseline."

Penny kisses her teeth. "Tsk. Tsk. Tsk. Fighting over a man."

Cash points. "You see that man. If you weren't getting married, you'd throw your hat in the ring."

"And I'd rip off your brim." I cackle. "But in all seriousness, I don't know how this is gonna go down. His sister has a friend up there, and I got the vibe that she has eyes for him too."

"Ah, hell. Never mind. I ain't got time to be in jail for beating up some random bitch."

"She didn't look like much of a fighter," I say.

"Don't judge a book by its cover," Penny adds.

"And if the dick is good...a bitch will fight over that."

Brent steps back into the car, and we go radio silent again—

bashfully quiet—during the short drive back to the house.

He unhooks the car a good ways away from the main home at what I perceive to be the guest house. A six-foot-three bearded man wearing a winter coverall jumpsuit meets him on the porch.

"Damn. They make 'em tall around here," says Cash.

"Yes, they do." I lean forward for a better look. "And from what I can see, this one is just as fine but a little older."

Cash giggles. "Cheers to a fun weekend."

Penny huffs. "Is that a wedding tent I see?"

Brent and the older gent shake hands and make an exchange of dollars and a plastic bag. He returns to the car and drives us to the front of the house.

Bellamy welcomes us inside, holding a tray at the door. "Blue mugs are coffee. Pink mugs are hot cocoa."

"Thank you," we say, picking our choice.

She says to her brother, "Take their bags upstairs." She smiles at us. "It doesn't matter what room he places your things in. Each room has a king-sized bed and its own bathroom. Welcome, ladies. I'm Bellamy."

"Cash. Short for Cashmere."

"Penny. Not short for anything. Just named for good luck, which seems to have run out this weekend."

Bellamy hugs her. "I don't know if Belise told you, but the weather caused a wedding to be canceled on the property. We're going to eat well, be merry, drink loads, and have a blast."

A caterer interrupts. "Ma'am, we've set up the dining room. Dinner will be ready to serve in thirty minutes."

"Thank you."

Brent comes back downstairs for another set of luggage.

His sister asks him, "How are the roads?"

"Picking up. The staff should probably get going before they form black ice."

Bellamy hands a check to the caterer. "You guys better get going before the roads ice. If I need help with the food tomorrow..."

"Just call me."

"Ladies, it was nice meeting you, but let's continue to get to know each other over some of the best stuffed shrimp and lobster bisque. Meet at the table in half an hour?"

"That gives me just enough time to get out of these clothes," says Cash.

We go upstairs and marvel at the infrastructure of the mansion being called a house. It's a monstrosity. Gorgeous. Modern. And classy.

We claim whatever room holds our luggage. Most of our bags are grouped together correctly, minus one or two small ones.

As we settle in, we tiptoe from room to room, passing along what belongs to who, and fawn at the rich décor. I can tell by the look on Cash's and Pen's faces that we are sharing the same thought.

What level of luxury have we crash landed into?

Chapter 3

Sam

"I hope your guests appreciate your kindness. I can't say that I would allow strangers to stay in my home. Blizzard or not."

"It's not something I would normally do, but my sense of discernment has never let me down. Besides, she was wearing three-hundred-dollar snow boots, a Cartier bracelet, and an Italian leather coat. The only killer she could be is a fashion killer."

"Oh, look." I stop Bellamy's fashion sermon. "They're finally joining us. Eight minutes late."

The leader of the pack enters the dining hall first. Decent attire. Black straightened hair that moves as she walks. Curvaceous body. Can't compete with mine but enough to turn heads.

The other two are cute. The darker one is cuter. Not over the top with labels like the ringleader. Shapely. Naturally pretty it looks like from where I'm seated. And I think she knows it.

"I'm Cashmere," she says.

"Sam." I acknowledge her with a nod.

"Are you the bride?" Claire asks.

"That would be me." The meek looking one raises her hand. "I'm Penny."

Claire gets up and hugs her. "I think I'm still a bride too. We'll see after this weekend. Come. Sit by me."

Bellamy taps her glass. "This holiday has been full of surprises so far. I love it, and I propose a toast. To twists and turns, new friends and old, we welcome those in need of warmth out of the cold." She raises her glass. "Happy holidays."

Everyone at the table salutes. "Cheers. Happy holidays."

The food from Claire's rehearsal dinner is exquisite. I expect nothing but the best from Bellamy. She always delivers.

Dessert is the top layer of Claire's wedding cake. She holds back tears in deep belief that this storm is an omen telling her to call off the wedding. Bellamy clocks in as the wedding planner and assures her the day will happen. Once Claire is calm, she hands her the knife.

"You do us the honor and cut your cake."

Almond flavor travels around the table as she slices.

"While she's doing that, I'm gonna make sure the den is nice and toasty for our first event of the weekend."

"What event?" the other bride asks.

"Tonight is storytelling night. We're going to pop some bottles, share some stories, then take our asses to bed because we have a long day tomorrow."

Belise asks, "Have you seen how hard it's coming down outside?"

Bellamy winks at me. "We'll show you how we do

around these parts." She presses the call button on the wall.

Brent answers, "Yes."

"Will you and Karl get the sleds ready tomorrow? Say around noon?"

"Sure. Anything else?"

"Yes. Come up to the main house and join us for breakfast in the morning."

He stutters. "I'll think about it."

We retire to the den. Champagne flows like the Mississippi River in the room. Bellamy pulls out a deck of UNO cards that are never dealt as we become heavily immersed in conversation.

The yellow bride loosens up the more she consumes. The other bride, who's been indulging with me all day, becomes a loud laughing machine.

"I have a story for you. I've been having an affair with my soon-to-be husband's best man. That's why this blizzard stopped my wedding. And that's why I came down here to "oversee" the venue. I can't face my fiancé."

The ladies take their turns guessing about her lover.

"Is it his brother?"

"Best friend?"

"Co-worker?"

A brief silence falls in the room until the high-pitched whistle of an osprey looking at us from the moon window, far up in the high ceiling, gets our attention.

I say to Claire, "That's an osprey looking down at you. They mean good fortune. I'd say everything is going to work out in your favor."

Claire slings her strawberry-blonde hair around and slurs the lyrics to a song no one in the room understands. Cashmere begins to giggle at her drunk rage and harmonizes the tune with her until they end it together in laughter.

"This one's cool," Claire slurs.

"Did we miss something?" My finger points around the room.

"She's singing, or at least trying to sing, 'I'm No Good.'" Cashmere pauses and wrinkles her face. "Amy Winehouse?" She gets up from the stacked pillows in front of the fire and sits at the foot of Claire's chair. "Girl, I know that album front and back. You are good, Claire, and you *ain't* married yet, so technically what you're doing isn't cheating."

"Ugh," the other bride fusses. "You will forever hang on to that ideology."

"Men do. Why shouldn't we?"

"Because we aren't men."

I interject, intrigued by their disagreement. "What's this argument?"

"My friend here doesn't like my way of thinking." Cashmere shrugs. "Men fuck anything before..." Her voice deepens. "And a lot of times after marriage. Almost every man I've been friends with claims whatever happens before they say those vows does not count. We are the ones who cut off access to other men when we find love. Men don't move like that."

"I like the way she thinks," Claire co-signs. "Are you married?"

"Divorced. My husband thought he was gonna play games during our marriage. I had to show him who the

real athlete was. And he couldn't take it
cackles. "And he still begs to come home."
for her glass.

I ask her. "Since you're steering the
tell us a story."

"Ugh, I have so many. Husband stories. Ex-hus-
band stories. Boyfriends before I got rid of my husband
—stories. Boyfriends I tried things with after I was no
longer married—stories. Can it be sexual?"

"By all means. We're adults here."

She tops off her glass and smiles at everyone
around the room. "Of all my pursuits, only one
has been able to match my nasty. And in all hon-
esty, I still don't know if I ever loved him, or
loved it." Her eyebrows wink. "Know what I
mean?"

Penny raises her hand. "I don't."

"Sure you do." Cash pities her friend. "I don't
know if I was in love with him, or *a-dick-ted. Dicmatized. Cocksessed. Bonesjonesed.* It was like he could read
my mind." She begins singing her words. "He'd move
to the corner when I wanted him to. Choke me at the
right time. Slap my titty when I didn't even know I
liked that shit."

The ladies and I snicker.

Cashmere lies back. "I've said too much."

I continue to pry. "I guess my next question is why
this one"—I point to Penny—"Doesn't know what
dicmatized means."

"Because she's a virgin," Cash blurts.

Penny throws a pillow at her friend.

"Get over it, Pen. You will thank me for these con-

ations in a week when you say I do." She throws the
pillow back. "I hope you've been taking notes. I'll be
expecting a thank-you card after your honeymoon."
She rubs her fingers together. "And cash is always nice."

"A virgin? How old are you?" I meddle.

"We're all thirty-one. How about you ladies?"

"Twenty-nine," I answer.

"Same," says Bellamy.

"Thirty-three," Claire tells us.

I clap my hands. "Well, if I could trade places with
you, Penny, I would. That first time should be magical.
My experiences haven't lived up to the hype. I'm like
your friend here. Of all my suitors, I've only had one
man to thrill me."

Bellamy sighs. "Not this again."

"Yes, this again."

Belise sets her drink on the coaster. "What's she
talking about?"

Bellamy shakes her head at me, but I say what I
know to be true anyway. "Panty Claus."

Cashmere's fascinated eyes meet with mine. "I beg
your finest pardon?"

"Panty Claus. He visited me in this house."

Penny draws closer to Belise. "This house is
haunted?"

"If the visitor brings you pleasure, *is it haunted*?"

Cashmere cackles like a banshee. "What on earth is
this woman talking about?"

Bellamy shushes me. "Pay her no mind. She's told
me this story a thousand times, and a thousand times
I don't believe her. Some myth she created in her
head."

"It *was* real. I had broken up with my boyfriend at the time and came over for my friend here to console me." I point to Bellamy. "We drank too much, and I ended up spending the night. Well, later that night, I said something along the lines of wanting to meet a man that would make me forget all about my ex, and in the middle of the night, I woke up to a strapping, shirt-less young man wearing a red Santa hat, and a white Zorro eye mask, and he had a long silverish-white col-ored beard."

"And?" they all ask, except for Bellamy.

"She claims no pants and no boots?"

"You remember." I smile at my good friend as my fingers trace the glass in my hand. "No pants. No boots. Just chocolate glory hanging like fruit on a tree, ready to be licked."

Cashmere clears her throat. "What exactly were those words you said again?"

"Cash!" the virgin shouts.

"What? It sounds erotic. And kinda dark."

"Well, if he visits my room, he's gonna get his ass kicked." Belise laughs.

"Nobody's getting visited by a Panty Claus. I've lived here fifteen years, and no such thing has ever vis-ited me." Bellamy finishes off her glass. "Sam...stop telling that ridiculous story."

Cashmere scoots next to me. "Wait. I have ques-tions. Did he say anything? How many times has he visited you?"

"Only once. And he didn't do much talking." I tap Cashmere's shoulder. "This one knows what I'm talking about."

Bellamy smacks my leg. "You ladies are welcome to stay down here as long as you like. I'm going to call it a night."

CHAPTER 4

CASHMERE

Belise and Penny sit at the foot of the bed in my room. We speak more with our eyes than our words, dodging the inevitable discussion of this Panty Claus until scaredy-pants Pen can no longer hold it in.

"So, are we all thinking Sam is whacko?"

"I don't. I think she's cool."

"Of course you do. You two hit it off like old chums having a drink at the bar."

"Pen, you have to learn how to read people. Some people make up stories to entertain a crowd. Think of it as her gift. To liven up the mood in spaces. Give people a laugh. You know...how I do sometimes."

"Right," Belise chimes in. "And you heard Bellamy. She lives here and has never seen this *Panty Claus*. Sam was pulling our legs."

"She seemed pretty believable to me." Pen's eyes stretch as if a lightbulb just went off in her head. "Can I sleep with the gun tonight? Just in case."

"No, Pen. You'd have us doing a ten-year bid with

your trigger-happy fingers. Let's go to bed so in the morning you can see how silly you're being right now."

"Fine. But keep your ringer on. If I scream, you better come running and blasting."

Belise rolls her eyes then locks them with mine. I hide my sniggle and giggle beneath my hand. They leave my room, and when their doors close, Belise texts me.

'You up for playing a trick on her?'

'You know I am.'

'What'd you have in mind?'

'When everyone in the house is asleep, I'll grab what I can find downstairs and report back.'

'Cool.'

My eyes can't stop staring at the family's initials embroidered on the bathroom towels as I remove my makeup and change out of my dinner attire. The thickness of the cotton shouts, "We have money." The added family crest adds a not-so-subtle touch to convince you further.

I return to my bed and give everyone time to fall asleep. I squirm to find a comfortable spot to call mine for the next few days when a red folded note with a candy cane seal sticks out on the dresser.

"That wasn't there before," I murmur, looking around the room.

A grin covers my mouth.

Pen must have heard us. She's trying to get one over on us the way we're planning to get one over on her.

"I'll show you." I break the seal and read the note to myself. *"Are you sugar, or are you spice? Are you naughty, or are you nice?"* I chuckle, look at my reflection in the mirror, and hold in my laugh when I answer, "I'm always a naughty bitch."

The card tickles me, but the mischievous side of me can't stop my wild imagination overflowing with ideas on how we can prank the innocence out of Little Miss Goody Two-Shoes.

❄

I roll side to side in bed until the house is still. At a quarter past midnight, I tiptoe down the stairs to raid the rooms behind the closed doors that lead into the dining hall.

"Shit," I whisper, twisting the knob of the first door that won't budge.

I try a second door and get the same result, so I ease past the dining hall and wind up next to the pantry. Red linens that were on the table at dinner catch my eye, sticking out of a rolling tray past the fridge.

We can use that as a cape and whipped cream for a beard.

Smugly, I purse my lips, pleased with myself for what I've found as I slide into the pantry to collect the supplies. The shelves are overstocked, making it impossible to find the cream. My mind re-scans the house for anything white that I could swipe and put back when my heart nearly bursts out of my chest.

"Oh shit," I gasp.

Afraid to turn around, I raise my hands and say,

"Sorry. I got hungry. I hope you don't mind my searching for snacks in the middle of the night."

"I see a snack in front of me." A deep baritone voice sends chills down my spine.

I drop the tablecloth and spin toward the manly voice on my toes. My lips part and my heart pounds in my chest as I meet eyes with the myth. The man. The legend. Panty Claus, in all his glory, just like Sam described him, minus one detail—twinkling eyes behind a white mask. But she got everything else right. Red hat. White beard. Muscular chest. Swinging dick. Cocoa skin.

Chapter 5

Cashmere

Mesmerized that he's real, I stand there in silence with my eyes caught in his seductive gaze below the downlights.

"You dropped something," he says. "Turn back around and pick it up."

"Excuse..."

"Shut the fuck up," he orders boisterously. "Turn around." His voice then softens. "And pick it up."

I shiver as I obey his order, turning slowly so as to not make a sudden move. I bend at the waist, and my hair sweeps the floor. Manly hands cuff my hips and guide my body backward.

His length greets me and grinds against my satin panties. The friction causes them to rise between my cheeks, exposing my ass.

Claus lets out a pleased sigh at the sight of my skin then smacks one cheek. "You can do better than that," he says, smacking my cheek harder. "Yes. Look at that rippling effect." He smacks it again. "Naughty girls get punished. I hear you're on my list."

I'm stunned by my quick arousal, feeling warmth shoot through me like a heat seeking missile. In shock, I become speechless, managing to only whine a screechy note for my answer.

Smack! Smack! He vigorously punishes both cheeks.

"Ooh," I moan.

"I felt that pussy flinch. You are a naughty one." He groans.

His rough hands tightly squeeze my bum then slide my panties to the side. I twist my head to look at him, but he stops me, pressing into my lower back.

"Did I tell you to turn around?"

"No." My voice trembles when I answer.

A low groan roars behind me, and he fists my panties into a firm ball. I squeeze my pussy as tight as I can, but his grip and control wedge them between my folds and deliver a friction so intense and satisfying, I feel a trickle of wetness spurt out from the thrill.

"Holy hell." I sigh.

He smacks my ass, gentler this time. "I can take you there."

A sinister laugh registers behind me. He grinds me while shifting my panties creased inside my folds.

"That pussy is nice and wet. But I can make it wetter. Do I have your consent?"

"Yes. Yes, I consent."

He forces his finger inside my hole. His rough manner takes me to heights I have craved, and I savor this moment, yearning for more, as more is delivered like I can't be satisfied, but hope that isn't true.

Deep, his fingers reach into my abyss. Curated thrusts rub my pussy, soaking his hand as he plunges four fingers inside of me, pulling my panties to near shreds as he uses it as a bonus feature.

'Fucked with my own panties. I've never.'

"Mmm. I'm gonna stretch this little pussy."

I feel the soreness swelling, still wanting him to bring me more pain that will delve into pleasure. "Yes. Please. Stretch me, Saint Big Dick."

Abruptly, he releases me and lifts me by wrapping my hair around his fist. The back of my head rests on his shoulders. I begin to beg to feel his big dick, but he shuts me up with a hand wrapped around my neck, gripping the sides of my throat like a ball. His teeth graze my ear, and the furriness of his beard warms my shoulder, but I hold still, waiting for him to give me what I want.

"The name's Claus."

"That may be, but I call 'em how I see 'em."

"Disobedient with a smart mouth. Maybe you need to be choked another way."

Claus's hand leaves my throat. The other turns me around and forces me to my knees by way of hair in his grasp. For a quick second, I get an up-close flash of his twinkling eyes that follow me to the floor.

"Open up that filthy mouth," he orders.

My pussy throbs as I greedily welcome him. I close my eyes as he guides my head forward and strokes his dick down my throat. Saliva drips on my nightgown and sends a chill to my chest while I take the punishment of him face fucking me like he'd been dreaming of what it would feel like to glide across my tongue.

I tap his thigh for a rest, but he ignores it, forcing me to withstand the discomfort. I look up at him and challenge his power, pretending I can keep going when I'm in need of air.

"That's it. Breathe through your nose."

I push through and reach for the shelf, resting my hand on a plastic cup of fruit cocktail neatly stacked in rows. I pull one from the stack, and he pauses, buried deep in my throat. His fist eases up his grip slightly. His other hand cups my face.

I widen my mouth, stick out my tongue, and trace it across his balls. His thigh muscles tighten, and he trembles, finally releasing me.

My shoulders slouch, and I catch my breath. He lifts my face with his fingers pinching my chin.

"Were you trying to make me cum before I felt that tight pussy of yours?"

I roll back on my knees. "Well, it's waiting." I slide the fruit over and peel off the plastic. "Pineapple makes pussy taste extra sweet." I pick one out and swallow it. "I'll let you be the judge."

"I will when I'm done with that messy mouth of yours."

He steps forward and bends his knees. Towering over me like I'm the back wheels of a wheelbarrow. I'm in an uncompromising position—on my knees, leaning back, hair in a death grip at the nape, and a mouth full of dick trying to travel down my esophagus like it's the yellow brick road.

"Ah," he whines and pulls out. "One more time."

I exhale and swallow him. Stimulated by his dominance. Drenched and sticky between my yearning legs impatiently waiting to be parted.

Claus exits my mouth, pinches one nipple, and slaps the other. My eyes grow wide, beginning to believe he is a ghost—a ghost who knows what I like.

He slaps both my breasts then grins. "I wish I had more time with you."

"What do you mean?"

"It's time for you to be Santa's little helper."

"I hope that means you're about to ride me like I'm one of your reindeer.

He slides my panties down my legs as he falls to his knees and lifts my left leg over his shoulder. I hold onto his hat and watch him clean up the mess he caused with his nose pressed against my clit, and his lips licking me clean.

He looks up at me. "Naughty bitch with a tight pussy that tastes good. I'm gonna call you Vixen."

I cock my head back and play with my nipple while the other hand holds myself up, gripping on the red velvet cap. I could collapse from the sensation of his tongue play —swiping left and right and in a circle around my slit, but I'm confident I won't fall with his hand rubbing on my ass cheeks, securing my pussy to his face.

His tongue is buried so deep inside my pussy that his beard tickles my asshole. I just about lose it when one of his fingers joins the party, thrusting up and down my aching walls.

"More," I beg of him.

Three fingers add more pressure, but I'm still not there.

"More," I beg again.

He lowers my leg and lifts me up against a freezer in the corner. He reaches under his hat and tears a condom wrapper with his teeth. Neither one of us blinks as he rolls it down his dick.

"Umph," I scoff at his tip penetrating my walls.

I hold onto his broad shoulders, breathing heavy and low with my back glued to the cold freezer like pasta sticking to a wall. The thrill and fear of someone walking in on him serving me good dick removes the boredom I thought I would face coming up to the mountains. I am in heaven in the middle of nowhere on a wild, dangerous ride, making this trip I once dreaded worth it. Abso-fuckin-lutely worth it.

I focus on the way his mouth is parted as he takes my goodies with curved thrusts to my corners and sturdy strokes that make me squeal when I cum.

"You look like a Beyonce type bitch. Get on mute." He leans forward and holds my lips shut between his teeth.

I breathe in his cologne. He breathes in my sighs. My ass screeches on the stainless steel. The shelf next to the freezer vibrates. Shortly after, so does he.

Claus wraps my leg around his back and squishes up against me so tight we become one. His head falls to my shoulder, and I exhale, holding in my scream, and release a soft moan.

His hand brushes my skin from my waist up to my neck. He silences me, asphyxiating my panting breaths and moan with a firm hold.

The intensity heightens between my legs, and my body feels explosive from my feet to my upper back. I can hear my heart beating against the steel and in my head. It's loud, just like how I feel.

Claus jolts within my walls, grunting against my neck like a wolf closing in on its prey. My fingers dig deep into his back, and his muscles twitch when he finally takes a breath.

"I enjoyed you, Vixen." He lowers me to my feet.

"I enjoyed you, Claus."

He gives me a gentle kiss. It's magical and sweet. Intense yet dreamlike.

He slides out of me, but I try to hold onto him with dewy hands slipping from his back to his shoulders.

"Turn around," he tells me.

My fingers lose their grip. I let go of him and obey his command, waiting to feel him press against me, impatient for his touch to reconnect with my body. But seconds go by, and I grow antsy, in need of his rough hands to indulge me.

My rebellious nature challenges his authority, and I turn around to touch his smooth skin to fill the void. But what I find is a shut pantry door, and I'm the only one standing in the confined space. Claus is gone.

I look around, holding myself, freaking out that I'm going crazy, as if a possessed spirit took control of my body.

Am I being taught a lesson because of the prank I was plotting on Pen? Did my mind get the best of me? Did I imagine this?'

I pick up the tablecloth, fold it, and place it back in the bin. I put my hand on the door and suddenly recognize my panties are gone.

I search for them in the bin, near the freezer, and on the shelves. All I find is the cup of fruit I opened.

I carry the cup up to my room, lock my door, and lean against it, full of myself in a haze.

When I return back to reality, I message Belise.

> No luck finding anything. Let's try again tomorrow. Good night.

CHAPTER 6

BELLAMY

Belise, Penny, and Sam sit in the den, enjoying coffee, by the time I make it downstairs in the morning. I open my mouth to ask where the other two ladies are when Claire pops in from around the corner with a canister of sugar.

"Coffee?" she offers.

"I should be the one offering you coffee. How long have you all been down here?"

Belise twists her hand. "Roughly twenty minutes. Give or take."

"Is everything alright with Cashmere?"

"She begged us to let her sleep in. I can go wake her if you want."

"No need." Cashmere plops down the last step, stretching her arms. "It's been an eventful twenty-four hours. I needed my beauty sleep." She yawns. "Good morning, ladies."

"Good morning."

"Mornin', Sunshine." Claire raises her mug.

"I hope you're all rested, because the games begin when the sun sits above the house. Originally, I thought let's do it at noon, but the storm is reported to let up for two hours then come down hard again for the rest of the day. That gives us time to enjoy breakfast and lounge around for about two hours." I clap my hands. "So, I'll go set the table."

I bake quiche and pastries, scramble eggs, broil buttered toast, and griddle pancakes. I grab a few linens from the pantry, lay the spread on top of it, then make a final trip inside the pantry to gather the jellies and jams. I scowl at them tipped over on the shelves.

The house manager wouldn't have left them like that.

Next to the shelves, smudges on the freezer puzzle me.

"I need to have a word with Mae about this when she comes back."

Back at the table, my guests are sharing the dishes over conversation like a lively bunch. I place the preserves at both ends of the table and notice Cashmere looking around as if she's lost something.

"Everything alright?" I ask her.

"Yeah. Everything's fine." She glances at the wall behind her. "Anyone else have one too many last night? Besides Claire?"

Claire giggles as if she's still buzzing.

Penny answers, "I slept like a baby last night, so it's a possibility *I* did. And good thing too, 'cause Sam here had me afraid to sleep in my room by myself."

Sam laughs. "Did I? I didn't mean to."

I scoff. "I told you not to tell that story."

"It's not a story. It's the truth." Sam fans her hand at Penny. "Forget what I said last night. It was a one-off, and that happened years ago. I waited for Mr. Claus to pay me a visit last night. At some point, I passed out and didn't experience a thing." She taps the table. "You have nothing to worry about."

Penny raises a brow. "And how do you know that?"

"Because I've been waiting for five years to offer myself to him and let him have his way with me. I guess he only strikes once."

Belise snickers while biting on toast. "You mean to tell me," she says, struggling to swallow to say what's on her mind, "even a man-ghost wants to dick and dash?" Her snicker turns into a snort. "Women just can't win."

All of us cackle at the truth then quiet down when Brent walks in with Karl on his heels.

"Yes. Lawd," Belise says, staring at my brother.

"Who are they?" Claire asks.

I introduce my brother and the land's hand, Karl, to everyone. They all speak to them with soft voices and steal glances between the two of them with no shame.

"Please, join us." Sam pulls out the chair next to her.

"We'd love to, but Bell has us working this morning to make your stay here a memorable one. We just came in to say good morning and grab a plate to go."

"Any luck getting our car to crank?" Belise asks Brent.

Karl responds. "Got it to crank a few hours ago. I'll have the dents pulled out by the time it's safe for you ladies to get back on the road."

Penny sighs in relief. "Thank you."

"My pleasure, ma'am. See you ladies in a few hours."

I help put food on two plates while each one of the ladies sparks conversation with the only men around. Their eyes become bloodthirsty, and flirtation steams the room. Batting dough-like eyes, pursed lips, big smiles, hair tosses, and fake laughs remind me of survival of the fittest. Except, in this case, it's survival of the come and get it.

"Bye, Brent." Belise waves.

"Bye, Karl." Claire tips her mug.

"Bye, Brent. Bye, Karl." Sam slurps on her coffee.

"Bye, Brent." I shove the plates in his hand.

CHAPTER 7

BELISE

Looking cute in the snow was a part of the original plan, so Bellamy arranging activities to entertain us is fine with me.

I stunt on these heauxs in my ivory snow-suit ensemble, with matching boots, fur hat, and wide-rimmed ski goggles. As I'm primping in the bathroom mirror, Cash enters my room.

"I'm in here!"

Her suit swooshes as she strolls in. "Okay, Diamond." She teases me, giving me a once-over.

"She ain't the only one who stuns in white." I twirl. "Did that extra half hour do you some good?"

"It did what it was gonna do." She traces the K monogram on the towels. "I have this thing that once I'm awake, I never fully go back to sleep. So, I basically closed my eyes while my brain kept saying *get up, get up*, until I finally did." She watches me finish putting on my makeup. "How'd *you* sleep in a strange bed last night?"

"Great, surprisingly. Felt like I was sleeping on a pillow of clouds." I blot my lips. "When I woke up, I thought, '*Oh shit I left Cash hanging last night,*' then I saw your text."

Her eyes wander around the room. "Guess it was a good thing I didn't find anything, then, huh?"

"Well, I found something."

Her eyes meet mine in the mirror. "What?"

"I went to freshen up before bed, and this was sitting on my sink."

I hand Cash a white note sealed with a mistletoe sticker on the edges. She reads it aloud.

"Are you sugar, or are you spice? Are you naughty, or are you nice?" Her eyes light up. "I had one of these on my dresser too."

I scoff. "Ha. You think Pen is on to us and reversing the play?"

"I doubt Pen has it in her."

"Maybe Sam, then?"

"Could be." She looks away and shrugs. "How did you answer?"

"I laughed at it and said none of your fuckin' business. How'd *you* answer?"

"I said naughty."

I snicker in her face. "Of course you did." I slide on my gloves. "I'm ready."

We go outside and stay warm around a pit of fire the men on the land prepared for us. My red lips pop against the pure white backdrop of snow-covered mounds decorating the Kingsburd's land.

"Pose!" Cash yells, taking my picture while we wait for Bellamy to join us.

"Nice outfit." Sam offers a compliment. "Have you

ever heard you shouldn't wear a blue bathing suit in the pool?"

I don't answer her, sensing the venom in her tone.

"Never wear white in a blizzard."

"You could have stopped at nice outfit."

Bellamy, stunning in her trendy, mauve-colored snow gear, hands her brother a red flag. Now that she's stolen the spotlight, she explains the rules for the first obstacle.

"You all know how races work. Well, we're going to split into two teams of three and race down this hill. Bride versus bride. Claire, Sam, and myself versus you three. Karl will select who will battle who and help secure us in the sleds. Brent will keep track of who crosses the finish line first. Best two out of three wins this round! Let's go!"

The girls and I huddle at the opposite end of the fire. Cash uses her fitness knowledge to explain a winning strategy regarding weight.

"Penny's fuller figure should hand us the win against Claire, who we're banking won't make it across the finish line."

Suddenly, she loses focus.

I snap my fingers. "Earth to Cash. Where'd you go just now?" I look over my shoulder and see she's staring at Karl.

Her eyes sparkle. "Does he look like he can fuck to you?"

"Yes. The man is a looker. And he's quiet. Men who keep to themselves can usually dick you down. Now what does that have to do with us winning?"

Cash grins, never shifting her eyes away from Karl.

"Nothing. As I was saying, you and Sam will be a close call, so when it's my turn, you need to push me to the edge before Bellamy. And lean forward as far as you can. Got it?"

Penny and I nod.

Karl straps Penny and Claire in the sleds first. He blows the whistle, and Cash and I race to get her to the edge. She takes off screaming, then cursing, then screaming again. We laugh thunderously at her and Claire, flying down the drop with her hands up in the air while trailing Penny by a landslide.

Brent waves the red flag when Penny crosses. She hops off the sled and jumps up and down with the win while Claire takes her time to cross the finish. Looking at her, you wouldn't know she was the loser the way she celebrates at the bottom of the hill.

"It's cold as fuck out here." My lips quiver. "Can I forfeit my turn and just hang out by the fire?"

"Well, you guys won the first leg. If you win the next one, there's no need for the third."

Cash and I share a glance.

"You and me." Cash points to Bellamy. "Let's get this challenge over with so we can move on to the next one."

I ask her. "Confident you're gonna win?"

"Very." She pulls me close by my arms and whispers, "Use those thick legs of yours and push me to that edge with all you've got."

Karl secures her in the sled. I catch a whiff of manliness masked below cigar smoke and lighter fluid while he's hovered over her. Cash studies him closely like she's piecing together a puzzle. Her eyes tell a story, looking at the older gentleman, and his sneaky stares make me question if they know each other—or if they *want* to get to know each other?

Cash tugs on her pink toboggan. "Whoooo! Let's win this shit!"

Karl blows the whistle, and I push the sled with all my might. The muscles in my legs strain. I feel the burn, pressing my boots in the snow 'til they squish and leave prints in and out of the path from the previous push.

Cash hollers while her sled bounces down the steep hill, leaning forward as it flies down the slope like a jet skit would on water. Bellamy is silent, leaning forward like a professional who knows how to win.

I stand between Karl and Sam. They both cheer, but as for Karl, I can't tell if it's for Bellamy or Cash. I turn my head to look at him up close—to see what my friend finds so captivating about him besides his good looks.

His mouth drops open. I turn back to the race, then my mouth drops open. Bellamy's sled is skidding on the side of the wooden runners.

Brent raises the red flag as Cash cruises past him. She raises her hands in victory, clueless that Bellamy is snow kill behind her. She does a victory dance as Bellamy removes the strap and hops up from the snow, covered in it from head to toe, standing on both feet, and signaling she's fine. She kicks the sled, and the wood falls completely off, then everyone at the foot of the hill treks back toward us.

At the fire pit, we reconvene and discuss the next challenge—a snowmobile hunt.

"Karl and my brother have hidden mini Santas in the snow out back. Here's a hint—if you stumble upon a marked tree, you're close to finding one." Bellamy looks at her watch. "We have thirty minutes to find these fuckin' Santas because it's cold as shit out here, and we have one more challenge to go!"

Sam laughs out loud.

"That's the first time I've heard you curse since we've been here!"

"Freezing your ass off changes people! So, first things first—does everyone know how to operate a snowmobile?" She looks around. "Good. We have four bikes. Who wants to double?"

Sam warms up by hopping around. "Let's mix it up this time. Cash, you ride with me."

Penny follows her lead. "Claire can ride with me."

"This one's mine." Bellamy hops on the third. "Come on, fashionista." She roars her engine.

I hop on the last bike and take my time to catch up with the girls as flurries begin to fall. I assume Bellamy will turn everyone around, but she takes off at top speed into the woods.

I follow the sound of the engines surrounding me in search of a marker. The mobiles traveling ahead scuff up snow as they scurry along. Little Santa heads stick up from the ground. I collect three and still search for a marked tree.

The engines grow faint, and the snow begins to fall harder. I get turned around in the woods and silence my engine, hoping to hear the direction of the others.

Howling winds and thick flakes surround me. I

panic and search for skid marks my machine has left in the snow.

I crank the engine and follow the path at two miles an hour. Sounds of the other engines are obsolete, and my mind assumes the worst. I'm lost in the woods and alone.

I take out one of the Santa figurines I've found and kiss it. "I haven't celebrated Christmas in a long time, so I think I'm owed a wish. Get me out of these woods. Please."

The wailing winds begin to die down. The thick snowflakes turn back to flurries, and the sounds of the other engines become clear.

Crrr! A crunch in the snow startles me. Glistening eyes on a white jackrabbit find me on the verge of panic. It seems friendly as we stare at each other for a few seconds.

It blinks, turns around and takes a few hops, looks back at me, then hops toward the distant buzzing.

I follow it for yards and yards out of the forest, and relief overcomes me when my sight lands on the Kingsburd guest house where the car is being worked on.

I blow my horn and drive forward at full speed. Once I'm out in the open, I exhale the deepest breath and line up with the ladies revving their engines, kicking up snow dust.

"We were about to form a search party," says Cash.

Penny fusses. "Yeah, where the hell were you?"

"I got turned around when the snow started coming down hard."

"Did you at least find any Santas?"

"I found three. But never mind all of that. Can we go inside? Please?"

The wind picks back up as Karl and Brent take away the motor sleds. Bellamy leads us into the house through a backyard terrace door, but I hesitate and let everyone go inside before me.

With one foot inside and one foot still on the deck, I turn around to look back at the vast white field and forest-green trees.

Brent trots back to the house for the last bike. He cranks it and catches me staring at him. He smiles, and I smile back, then he reaches down and holds up one of the Santas.

I nod at him with widened eyes. He gets off the bike and brings them to me.

"I see you found three Kringles."

"More like they found me."

"Well, I put in a lot of work stashing them in the snow. I think you should at least keep one."

"I think I should too."

He places them in my hand then looks up. I glance above us and hold my breath. Our eyes meet, and he holds my gaze.

"Mistletoe," he says and pecks me on the lips. "Merry Christmas, Belise."

"Merry Christmas, Brent."

I swallow big, watching him drive away until he disappears behind the guest house.

"Belise! *You* coming!" Cash yells.

I close the door and say to myself, "It's a possibility."

CHAPTER 8

CLAIRE

"Look, I may have screwed up at everything we did today, but I'm fired up and volunteer to make coffee and hot cocoa," I tell the ladies huddled by the fireplace in the den.

"I don't know if I'm saying this now because we're thawing out, but I had fun out there." Cash takes off her hat. "Thank you, Bellamy."

"Yes. Thanks for getting us out of the house and showing us a good time under strenuous circumstances."

"My pleasure. I love putting smiles on other's faces." She looks at Belise. "Are you okay after your scare out there?"

"I'm fine. Just glad to be back inside."

Sam lays her gloves on the table. "Remember what I said about that white."

"What is she talking about?" Cash asks.

Belise mocks an identical smug look on Sam's face. "Nothing. She's talking about nothing."

Bellamy looks at me, confused.

I shrug.

"So, ladies..." Bellamy shifts the topic. "We have another thirty-six hours to go before this storm lets up. Then, probably another six to twelve hours until the roads are all clear. Tonight, I thought, after we enjoy our dinner, we could either have movie night, pamper night, spades night..."

"Spades?! Are you trying to get someone cut in here?!" Penny grimaces.

"Why would someone get cut over a game of spades?" Bellamy frowns.

The trio laughs.

"Obviously, you've never played spades. It can get pretty dark and competitive where we're from."

"Forget I said anything," Bellamy mumbles. "Cross out spades." She clears her throat. "We can also do a paint-n-sip, relax in the sauna and steam our pores, charades, karaoke, or truth or dare. I'm open to suggestions."

Cash raises her hand. "I vote we take a nap then reconvene."

"I'm with Cash," I say.

"But we should decide now so Bellamy can prepare," Penny adds. "I'd love to help you set everything up—help in any way."

"I'd love that."

"Then I vote Pictionary and watch a movie before bed."

The collective agrees to the idea.

Bellamy stands. "Great. Since we are spending Christmas Eve together, I have a surprise in store for you ladies tomorrow morning."

My phone buzzes in my pocket. "*What'dya* know.

Someone is finally returning my calls. If you'll excuse me."

I make myself scarce as the ladies chatter amongst themselves before disappearing into separate corners. With one shot of cocoa in my system and the camaraderie of powerful women who have given me advice and shown me care in the next room, I put on a brave face and take the call from my fiancé's best man.

"Hey."

CHAPTER 9

CASH

I peel out of my layers and lie across the bed. Cece's face lights up on my phone just as I'm about to close my eyes.

"Belise isn't answering her phone. How are y'all making it?" she asks.

"Pretty good, actually. It's almost like we're having the weekend we planned with y'all—but with strangers. How's everybody doing up there?"

She whispers, "I think I would rather be where you guys are. Naz has been drinking non-stop and starting fights with everyone. If we weren't snowed in, everyone would leave, and this trip would be a bust."

"Damn. We're having a good time on this end. Our host is gracious. She's been keeping us fed and busy. And the house is huge, nothing short of amazing."

"Rub it in, why don't you."

Belise barges in. "Something is up with this place."

"Hold on, Cece." I sit up straight. "What are you talking about?"

She plops on the bed. "Hey, Cece. Can we call you back? I need to have a word with Cash."

"No, you can't call me back. I'm having a horrible time over here. I wanna know *what's tea*."

"Fine." She exhales deeply. "There is something strange about this place."

"Mythical," Cash responds quickly. "Am I right?"

"Spooky."

Cece chimes in. "Spooky? Cash just said it was all kinds of amazing."

"Trust, the visuals are giving luxury and old money. But something weird happened to me when I was lost in the woods."

"What the fuck you doing getting lost in the woods?" Cece asks. "Damn, I'm in hell over here, and y'all are having adventures."

"I wouldn't call it an adventure. We were playing a holiday game, hunting for Santa figurines in the snow. The snow began to fall real heavy, and I couldn't see the path back to the house. I got scared and wished for the snow to clear up, and just like that"—Belise snaps her fingers—"it did. My tracks suddenly became visible, and I found my way back to the house."

"And that scared you?"

Cece's sarcasm through the phone pisses Belise off.

"*Yes!* It scared me. How about you get lost in the woods with hard winds and snow circling around you and tell me how it feels."

"Lise." I scowl at her. "I couldn't tell you were this bothered when we got back."

"Because I didn't want to be questioned by a bunch of people I hardly know."

"And I was just being facetious," Cece makes it clear. "I'm glad you're okay."

"Thanks." Belise sighs. "And sorry. I just don't know what to make of it." She looks at me with expanded eyes. "Should we tell her?"

I shake my head side to side.

Rustling in the background is heard on Cece's line. "Tell me what?" she whispers.

"About Panty Claus."

The rustling grows louder as Cece inches closer to her phone. A faint laugh can be heard on the line, then it grows louder. You can tell she's showing all her teeth when she asks, "What the hell y'all talking about?"

Belise repeats Sam's story to Cece. I add in the detail about the notes left in our room. She takes it all in and is quiet at first. Heavy breathing sounds from her line, then a small titter grows into a roaring laugh.

Belise and I laugh with her, but not as loud and not as long.

"That lady is fucking with y'all. She's pulling your legs."

"I think she's some sort of witch that made the snow trap me in the woods."

I tap her leg. "Is that what that white comment was about?"

"Yes. She told me you shouldn't wear white in a blizzard, and look what happened. Cece, you didn't see her face when she said it. *Andddddd*, I think she is leaving the notes in our rooms."

"She's not," I mutter below a yawn. "I have a confession." My arms stretch wide as I smile real big, chuckling. "I fucked Panty Claus last night."

Belise looks at me in disbelief. Cece hollers on the phone. Her screaming becomes distorted and distant for a few seconds. It's obvious she's running around the room, having a good laugh at my expense.

"Now, you're pulling my leg!" she yells in the background.

"It's why I couldn't find anything to use for our joke last night. I got *dick-stracted*."

"Where?"

"In the pantry. And yes, he used protection."

"You fucked a total stranger in a matter of seconds?"

I shrug. "It wouldn't be the first time. I like spontaneity."

Cece giggles. "I'm snowed in at the wrong house."

Belise shakes her head at me. Her shoulders drop like she's defeated as a heavy sigh deflates her chest. And she judges me with her eyes and a sour tone.

"Was it Brent?" she asks, her voice cracking with concern.

"Who is Brent?" Cece probes.

Belise answers her, "The host's brother. Certified babe. I studied him and Karl closely today."

"Who is Karl?"

I jump back in quickly. "The groundskeeper. A seasoned, certified babe. And I don't think it was either of them."

"Why not?"

"Neither of their eyes had a twinkle in them. Also, after the way we got down, one of them surely would have made some sort of notion toward me today." I suck my teeth. "I got zero traction."

"Well shit, it must be a butler or someone else who lives on the property," Cece adds.

"Or is it a ghost, like Sam said?"

"I'd rather have fucked the brother or Kyle, the Hand, instead of a ghost, Lise."

She leans toward me and transfers a ladybug from my leg to her finger. Slowly, she walks to the window and cracks it open to set it free. I curl up in bed as a chill sweeps through the room.

Cece clears her throat. "Inquiring minds wanna know...was it good?"

A smile gags me from answering.

"Judging from the look on her face, I'd say yes," Belise tells her with her arms folded.

I regain my voice. "Goddamn right it was good. If I was granted a wish like you were today, out there lost in the wilderness, I'd wish he was doing me right now. And maybe do you too." I flail my hands at her. "Because we all know you need it."

The words leave my mouth before I can bite my tongue. I'm aware I need to work on how blunt I can be, but sugarcoating shit has never been my schtick.

Belise is upset with my choice of words, of course. Her eyes cut through me as she storms out of my room.

'Is the look guilt because she knows I'm telling the truth that she needs to get laid, or is the look sheer anger for my courage in saying so?' I wonder.

"Jeez," I grunt, yawning again with Cece still on the line, hanging onto my every word.

"What?"

"I've said too much. Again. Pen's already making friends with the other girls because I told them she was a virgin, and the look Lise just gave me..." I take a deep breath. "The two of them might leave me stranded out here." I laugh it off. "I gotta go make this right. Talk to you later on tonight."

I stomp my feet on the bed after I hang up the phone. I want to sleep. I need rest, a recharge before the night's activities resume. But I'm too tired to move from the comfortable spot I've dug myself in.

I lie there, making faces out of the speckles in the ceiling, and begin to drift off. Just as I am about to fall in deep, a noise disturbs my journey.

I open my eyes and find Claus standing at my bedside. I swallow deep, watching him stroke the perfect weaponry—his shiny black dick standing at full attention in his hand. His twinkling eyes leer at me, and an impish grin is laced on his lips as he rubs his manliness to tempt me.

"I come bearing gifts."

I sit up. "You know, Claus, I like when I'm at eye level with a nice-sized pipe, where the up-close-and-personal visual of a man's thumb is traveling up the shaft in search of a pressure point before I suck him off and send chills down his spine."

"Vixen, Vixen, Vixen. Normally, I strike once. And only once. But I have been thinking about you, and you did wish for me to appear, so here I am."

I wet his head with a mouthful of lust. "And ready," I purr. "'Tis the season of giving."

I lie back. He needs no direction to slide my panties off my ass. He licks my pussy. Then my asshole. I plug my mouth with one fist and pull on the bed with the other. My ass is lifted in the air and in his mouth. The sucking carries on with perfectly timed rotation between one orifice to the other until I've stained the comforter.

His dick protrudes my slit, and I smile. I feared I'd never feel him again. Never have the pleasure to experience his sexual prowess once more.

He drills deep inside, holding my legs captive above my head with my hands trapped beneath my ankles. I feel all of him like this. Every inch. All the girth.

My pussy spits on his dick, and he growls low like a bear. I want to squeal. Shriek. Shout. But I hold it in below heavy, deep breaths of ecstasy I'll forever hold on to.

He releases my legs and presses one hand against my ass cheeks. The other massages my lubed asshole. A violent vibration takes over my body. I cum like I'm a tremor on a fault line.

Claus maneuvers his hand from my cheek to hinder the outcry I can no longer contain, drilling me harder and harder until it's time for him to exert himself.

He pulls me up and separates my lips with his thumb. I open wide and welcome the gift he came to bear inside my mouth where he fills it to his delight.

His thumb massages the side of my mouth. "I do hope I find you again."

I look up at him, silent, with a wistful smile, then excuse myself. I spit his bearings in the sink then look at myself in the mirror, stroking my own ego that I'm so good he came to see me twice.

I rinse my mouth and return back to the bedroom to tell him I hope I find him again too. But he's gone. Vanished into thin air. And so are my fuckin' panties. His souvenir.

I burst into Pen's room to decompress what Cash has shared. She's on the phone with her fiancé, so I'm quiet about my presence lurking in the background. She whispers something to him I can't make out clearly then tells him she loves him and will call him when we hit the road."

"Everything okay?"

"Yeah. Why do you ask?"

"I just left Cash's room. Thought I'd check in on you too."

"I'm fine. Enjoying myself, but also ready to get out of here."

"Same."

She stares at me like she's holding something back.

"You mind if I ask you something?"

Pen twists her mouth and flickers her eyes. "I could tell you wanted to. What's up?"

"Have you had a mysterious card show up in your room?"

"Yeah." She points to the dresser. "It was sitting there this morning."

I pick it up and read it. It's identical to the card Cash and I received.

My face falls flat. "And how'd you answer?"

"Sugar and nice. Why?"

"And nothing strange has happened to you?"

Pen rolls her eyes and sighs. "What's with you and Cash? First you two tell me not to buy into Sam's tall tale, and now *you're* acting weird, getting lost in the woods, and giving me the third degree about a note."

"Well, I changed my mind about what I said before. I think Sam could have been telling the truth. Something strange is definitely happening 'round these parts. And it depends on how you answer these cards being left in the room."

"If you say so. Are you gonna run this theory by Sam?"

"No. I'm only telling you and Cash." I look at the snow coming down so hard it's difficult to see the blueish-gray mountains in the backdrop. "If you notice anything strange, be sure and tell me. Okay?"

She nods and throws me the okay symbol with her fingers. "Exactly what happened to you out there, Lise?"

My eyes roam the vast lands outside. "I wish I could explain it."

CHAPTER 11

BELLAMY

I f the storm lets up, this is the last night my house will be filled with laughs and joy this season. My guests have made this Christmas feel like it did when I was a kid, but they'll soon leave and return to their corner of the world. If it weren't for them, I would have spent this holiday alone. And though we were brought together by a canceled wedding and a minor car accident, our time together has been magical, and I want to thank them for that.

Penny's help affords me time to make name place cards to add to the décor of unused flowers and candles selected for Claire's nuptials. R&B Christmas music sets the tone for the prepared feast. And the ladies are in the dining hall, rested and ready to party.

The spread on the table serves something everyone can enjoy. Beef, chicken, vegetable options, macaroni & cheese, sweet potato soufflé, and more wedding cake. We break bread, drink, and be merry, killing time with great conversation.

Sam taps her glass. "The forecast says the sun will shine tomorrow. The roads will be open for travel, and we'll go our separate ways. If Bellamy will allow me to speak for the both of us, thank you guys for making this weather emergency a fun one. Cheers."

We raise our glasses.

"My sentiments exactly. This house hasn't been this full at Christmas in five years. I was overjoyed when Claire called to book the estate for a Christmas wedding. And when she showed up the other morning and said people weren't coming because of the storm and put the wedding on hold, I was beyond hurt. But then, she asked if she could spend the storm here at the house in what was going to be her bridal suite, and I couldn't have been happier."

Sam says to Claire, "And I was supposed to have that room. But you deserved it—this time."

"Does that room have any special memories for you, Sam?" Claire winks at her. "I'm just kidding around. Nothing's happened to me in there."

"Oh, God. Not this again."

"Well, if you must know. That is the room where I was visited by Panty Claus."

My voice heightens, "Is that why you stay in there every time you visit?"

She grins with her glass up to her mouth.

"Don't take it personal, Sam. Maybe Panty Claus is a hit-it-and-quit-it type." Cash smirks. "You said it yourself, maybe he only strikes once."

Sam's eyes set on her glowing skin with fire in them. She's been serious about this story for years, so I attempt to cool the heat bubbling at the table and ask everyone to retire in the den.

The movie is on as background noise, completely

ignored as the ladies are heavily engaged in idle chatter from corner to corner.

"I have an announcement. I called things off with my fiancé."

The room takes a collective vow of silence.

"His best man called me last night, and I'm meeting him at the airport tomorrow." She crosses her fingers. "God forbid the forecast is accurate this time."

"How do you feel about your decision?" Penny asks.

"Relieved, actually. I wouldn't have been able to cut things off with him after I said my vows. I don't care about the judgment coming my way. I'm choosing my happiness, and it's with him."

Cash shouts out, "You're choosing good sex! Smart woman!"

"I beg to differ," Sam challenges her. "Choose money. Then good sex."

"I agree with Sam," says Penny.

Cash's eyes narrow in on her. "Now how would you know—let me stop. I've already pissed you off once."

"Well, congratulations, Claire."

She raises her bottle.

Belise clears her throat. "No shade, Bellamy. But is there any chance you have anything other than champagne and wine?"

"What do you have in mind?"

"Henny and Coke? Vodka? Moscato?"

"Excuse me while I check in with my brother. I'm sure he has at least one of those."

Brent insists on bringing the brown liquor to the

house. He and Belise pretend they're not looking at each other. I give them a few minutes to flirt before I step in between them and send him away before it becomes a battle of the peen to ruin my perfect holiday.

The change in alcohol livens up the house. The Christmas music disappears, and raunchy songs take over the radio. Cash removes a vase from a table in the hallway, and drags it into the den. She and Belise line clear plastic cups found in the pantry on each end and begin a game of shot pong.

Money somehow becomes a part of the game. The more I lose, the more intoxicated I become. It seems never ending how many times I hand over one and five dollar bills to Belise, who's had the best winning streak I've ever seen.

After hours of taking shots, singing karaoke, and gambling, Sam passes out on the sofa with Claire curled up at the other end. Penny abandons the party and retires upstairs, while Belise, Cash, and I dance into the night.

Around 12:30, the shot queens leave me as the last one standing. I quiet the room, cover the girls on the sofa with blankets, and take in the feeling tingling all over me, grateful for the happiest of holidays.

CHAPTER 12

BELISE

This trip to the wilderness isn't anything how I imagined it. After the eventful day, wads of information, loads to take in, and a long night of partying and singing, I treat myself to a hidden treasure in my luggage.

Its potency hits me as soon as I open the bag. I inhale the aroma and lift the joint to my mouth. I go into the bathroom to grab the robe hanging behind the door, and the annoying note catches my eye as I step into my wool slippers.

I flick it with my fingers. "I'm not any of these. Show yourself and explain what's really going on."

I throw on the thick, Sherpa robe, toss the riddle in the garbage, wrap a scarf around my neck, and step onto the balcony to take it all in but also decompress. I spark my line to heaven while freezing flakes fly past my face in the gentle winds and nestle myself in my own arms, close my eyes, and release the first cloud of smoke into the wild.

As I wait for the first drag to lift me to new heights, I laugh to myself about the unexplainable shit Sam and

Cash claim to have experienced. While the weed begins to work, theories form in my head. I begin to believe Sam recruited Cash to tell me that bogus-ass story.

"I bet that's what's going on," I mumble below my breath and take a second toke.

"What's going on?" a deep voice says behind me.

I cough on my smoke amid turning around, and reach for my pocket. "Shit." The gun is in my coat. "Where the fuck did you come from?"

"Never mind that. I'm always where I need to be. Now tell me what you think is going on?"

"I don't answer to you. Who the fuck are you anyway?"

"Claus," he says.

His eyes twinkle when he mentions his name. I give him a once-over and study his facial features behind an eye mask, Santa hat, and silver beard.

"Why are you here?"

"I'm granting someone's wish, and you asked me to show myself, so here I am."

I inhale a long drag and size him up. He's tall like the only two men I've seen on the property. His lips don't resemble Brent's from what I can see past the beard, and his eyes are a deeper brown when they aren't glistening in the light.

"So what's your deal?"

"What's your desire?"

"None of your business."

"It is tonight, feisty, difficult one." His villainous laugh teases me. "I love a challenge. Think I'll call you Comet."

"Excuse me?"

He grins. "Yes. Comet. You're stubborn. You think you're tough. And I'm gonna make you cum fast."

I flick the ashes of my joint on the bricks. "I didn't give you consent to do such a thing."

"You will."

"You seem sure about yourself."

"It's what I do—deliver."

He steps forward and takes the joint from my hand, inhales a toke, and blows the smoke in my mouth. I hold it with puffed cheeks as his gaze holds mine, and his gleaming eyes attempt to put me in a trance.

He adds to his seductive charm with erotic word-play. "I bet that pussy is so tight you could suck a drag with it."

I jitter from the cold winds whirling around us. "Oooh. Listen to you. I heard you know a lot about pussy."

His warm hand caresses my cheek. "I can show you better than I can tell you. But you have to consent."

He kisses me, confirming he isn't Brent.

"Here's a challenge for you. Make me cum quick, like you said, so I can call it a night. You have three minutes."

"I'm no three-minute man."

"And I'm done playing games for tonight."

He places the joint between my lips. "Finish that off while I finish you off."

With one hand, he turns me around and presses me up against the iced bricks. Claus lifts my gown. His beard brushes the center of my ass while I inhale what's left of the joint.

A cold breeze cuts my bare skin, and I shiver. The

wet warmth of his tongue tastes my peach, and I drop the joint into the snow.

Mentally, I climb an invisible wall as the pfff takes me into the clouds. Physically, I'm losing all control from the mix of sensation and intoxication—high in every aspect. From having my ass eaten out, to the lift of the weed strong enough for a man but, at this moment, made for this woman at the *correct* improper time.

Claus grunts as he eats my asshole like he's been waiting for dinner. His backshot kisses fill me with heat, enough to sustain Jack Frost nipping on my toes.

His tongue slips down to my pussy lubed from the toss. He shows bias to my clit with his finger, pressing and rubbing it like a speed demon on a track.

I dig into the inches of snow mounted on the top brick with both hands. My back arches from the stimuli, feeding myself to him on the verge of a fit.

"That's one," he grouses, holding my clit between two fingers as I tremble against the ice.

I moan and moan and moan. My throbbing pussy suddenly *does* have all night, wanting more and more of what he came to give.

"I completed your challenge with minutes to spare. Shall I continue, Comet?"

I nod. "Yes. You fuckin' betta."

The crumpling paper alerts me, but he's too quick with it before I can back out. The cold plastic infiltrates my walls. My body tenses at the rough penetration pounding my island like a storm surge.

He steadies me with one hand lodged in the center of my back. I'm stationary, welcoming this fabled creature to pummel my pussy the way it needs it. The way I need it.

His lashing warms me in the dead of night in unfavorable conditions. And as he said, he delivers...and delivers well.

The buildup of his eroticism and thrusting hips begins to escape me. Claus pulls my hair and breathes on my neck.

"Don't you dare. You hold it."

I cry out with stunted breaths. "I can't."

His motion stops. His dick holds still. His voice vibrates throughout my body. "I said hold it."

I squeeze my pussy wrapped around him planted deep in my soil.

"That's it. Hold it for me, Comet. Just a few seconds more."

I whine, and I shiver. I'm tense all over, wanting him to tighten up on his backstroke in my good stuff so I can cum again. The pressure of his dick resting at the top of my pussy stifles me. It moves, but barely, pressing into my cavity just enough to satisfy me but not enough to withdraw what I'm holding.

My hands begin to melt the ice below my fingertips, and I moan against the slush sticking to my face. He tugs on my scarf and cuts off my air then strokes me fast and deep. My mouth opens wide, gasping for air, while I cum like fireworks a week ahead of the New Year.

He senses my explosion winding down and releases his grasp of the scarf. I gulp in huge amounts of air, breathe out, and form a large cloud of fog that floats above us.

Claus presses my hips and unloads his weapon in

my pussy. It's so cold outside, I feel the warmth of his seed heat inside the condom.

He slides out of me. "Thanks for the good time, Comet."

I collect myself from the bricks with a wet nightgown sticking to the heat formed from my sexual escapade. It takes a few pulls to free myself as it attempts to re-ice, but I manage then turn around to thank Claus.

"You sneaky bastard," I grumble into the bitter air.

Because Claus has abandoned me and taken my panties with him.

CHAPTER 13

PENNY

I'm sloshed.

The singing, the drinking, and the games have given me a night to remember. It's not the party I expected for my sendoff, nor is it being shared with the people I know and love. But this newfound group of characters has dug a special place in my heart.

I nearly piss myself from the number of drinks I threw back. I wake up in the middle of the night and dance my way into the bathroom, singing a song performed at karaoke, and handle my business.

I look outside my window to see if the snow has eased up. It's not falling as heavily as it was during the party, and hope encompasses me that we'll get back on the road later on today.

A draft chills my face as I look out into darkness with dandruff-like flakes falling on the sill. I close the drapes and walk back to my bed when the card Belise questioned me about falls on the floor.

I read it and laugh about the nonsense the girls have been trying to sell me.

"I've always been nice. But just once I'd like to be

naughty so I can know how to please my husband after we're married," I say to myself, carrying the note back with me to the bed.

"Allow me to show you," a deep voice whispers in the room.

A tall entity in a Santa coat and velvet red hat tilted to the side appears near the window. His eyes twinkle at me behind a white mask laced across a chocolate face. His silver beard shines in the dim light below pearly white teeth smiling at me.

He steps forward, and I shriek. The note falls from my hands onto the bed as I reach for my phone.

"Don't be afraid." He takes another step closer. "I'm here to fulfill your wish."

His steps are long strides as he's closer to me in the blink of an eye. Half-naked...handsomely half-naked.

"I can show you how to please your husband." His hand wraps around his dick. "Would you like to learn from me?" His eyes sparkle brighter as they gaze down on me. "Say the words, 'I consent.' You'll be happy if you do. I give you my word."

My eyes try to roam away from the long, erect, chocolate tower calling to me from below the hem of his coat.

"Who and what am I giving my consent to?" I ask him when I should be asking *where are the rest of your clothes?*

"Name's Claus. At your service."

"The one poor Sam can't stop talking about. You tend to leave your prey broken-hearted. And I'm engaged." I show him my ring. "I'm also a virgin. I've promised myself to my soon-to-be husband."

"You can still be a virgin when you marry your beloved. I won't penetrate—unless you change your mind."

I watch him stroke his dick in my face, and I feel a tingle between my legs. "Sounds too good to be true," I say, struggling to take my eyes off the way he jerks himself.

"I'm only here to grant your wish and show you how to please your man. But I'll please you just the same." His glimmering gaze holds mine. "Say you consent to learn from me."

A sense of calm overpowers me. "I accept your teaching. I consent."

My body relaxes, though my heart rate is up exponentially, beating powerful and fast the moment his hand caresses my face.

"You have a very inviting mouth." His finger parts my lips. "Lesson one. I'm going to fuck it now."

My eyes widen at his candor.

"Trust me, your husband will love a good girl that knows how to properly suck a dick."

His coat inches higher as his penis replaces his finger in my mouth. He begins slowly, as if he cares, guiding my head forward at the same pace he bucks his hips.

"Let it drip," he says to me.

I stop trying to swallow the moisture his movement is producing in my mouth. I follow his order and let my saliva drip down my chin but catch some of it, which makes a slurping sound.

"Yes," he groans. "Yes, my good girl. Just like that," he whispers. "Just like that."

I close my eyes as he continues shoving his length down my throat.

"Do this three to four times a week. Nod if you understand."

I nod.

"A man wants to be awakened like this at least once a week."

He thrusts forward against my cheek and slaps it. "Nod that you understand."

I do as he says, while being crossed between wanting him to stop because of the degradation I feel of allowing him to do such a vile act to me, but also not wanting him to stop, like I have something to prove to him—and myself.

The more he thrusts, I become stimulated vaginally. The more he talks to me in that low, considerate tone, I become enthused mentally. I feel my pussy growing wetter and wetter, throbbing for him to experiment on me and short change what I've promised to give my soon-to-be husband.

The thrusts become intricate. Exploratory and vigorous. His demeanor switches from caring to selfish, and my mouth becomes a warm cave for him to enjoy to his own liking.

He gives me a moment to catch my breath. "Lesson one is complete. You're doing good."

I look up at him and exhale. "My name is Penny."

"I know your name." He lifts my face by my chin. "But I'm gonna call you, Cupid.

"Why?"

"Because you're selfless and in love." He leans down and kisses me gently. "Lesson two. Lie back for me."

I shiver when he hovers over me. "You promised you wouldn't penetrate."

He slides his finger back in my mouth. "Look at how you already miss me dragging on your tongue." He pushes his hips forward and lifts my head to meet his tip. His dick trembles as he rolls it around my mouth. "Shhhh. Don't speak unless I ask you a question. Now, where were we?"

"Lesson two."

"That's right. Do as you're told."

A moment of regret charges through my body while the one throbbing part thumps like a heartbeat. I shock myself, loving how dirty he's talking to me. I feel ashamed. Nasty. Vulnerable. Sexy.

I lick my lips to taste him again. He circles my tongue and groans. The essence of him enjoying me makes me yearn to feel him inside of my body. For a moment, I convince myself to grant him the first feel of my pink underworld. I wonder if my husband would know I've been tainted and touched if I extend my consent.

He rolls back with his dick dragging across my thigh. He rips the seam of my panties and slides them from under me.

His finger swipes my pussy. "Let's see if you really are sugar." He licks his finger clean. "Mmm. You do have a sweet pussy." He rubs my entrance with the precision of a specialist. "I think I'll have some more."

The massage to my labia becomes addictive and insatiable. I reach for his shoulder and get lost in his gleaming eyes, searching for the right words to tell him how I like seeing him play with my pussy, then watch him lick my essence from his fingers like he can't get enough of me. How appreciative he appears to sample me. How my mind also feels like it's being fucked watching him enjoy me.

My sight blurs, and my body grows tight. The muscles in my legs ache from my pointed toes curled like shrunken plastic wrap, and my head turns woozy.

"We're still at the beginning, Cupid."

His fingers manipulate my control, and he continues to drain my pool. I vibrate like a ringing clock as my excitement drips to my ass. Claus sucks two fingers clean.

"Your taste test indulges me for a full plate." His face slides between my legs. "Look at that perfect canvas." He sucks from my cup and groans. "Your fiancé is lucky I don't take his precious gift you've been saving for him." His tongue flicks my clit, and I jolt. "It wants me to stretch it." He sucks on it like he's emptying the juice from a ripe strawberry. "So do you." His assertiveness nearly sways me. "Say you've changed your mind and want to give it to me," he says, looking up at me with a twinkle in his eye.

I moan. "I...I...d... No."

He grins. "Very well. I'd be a fool not to ask. It's so pretty." His fingers glide up and down the sides of my slick pussy with the softest caress. "Pink and brown is the best color combination there is."

His words weaken me just as much as his tongue. I nearly fold and let him break me.

At every exit, I flinch, wanting to explore more, holding my breath and my tongue to keep from saying the words that would have me break my promise.

The magic of his tongue licking and flicking me, his lips sucking me, and his mouth cupping me sprawled across the bed frees my inhibitions. The sensation and combination of all three serving me simultaneously with a finger rubbing my bud sends convulsions throughout my body.

Claus flips me over on my stomach. I become nervous that I'm not on defense, and I look back at him over my shoulder.

He unzips his jacket. "Lesson three."

"I still haven't changed my mind."

"You might." He pulls out a long, leather black stick with a heart on the end. "Turn around."

"What lesson is this?"

He grunts. "Submission."

He smacks my ass gently with the whip. I shrill at the excitement. The next smack hits a little harder. I bounce slightly on the bed.

"On your knees."

I do what he tells me when the next smack stings my cheek. I flinch—so does my punani—and I clench the sheets with both hands. *Smack!* Another strike stuns me.

"Look at me," he orders.

I look at him over my shoulder.

Claus runs the heart end of the stick across my folds. "I could go harder, but this is a simple lesson. If your husband explores this world with you, he'll give you a safe word. "Do you understand?"

"Yes." I sigh. "I like what you're doing right now, Claus."

He rubs the leather against me harder between my slit. "There's so much more I want to show you."

He pulls out a black tassel and brushes it across my butt. My hips gyrate back and forth, and my hole shrinks and expands, yearning for him to show me.

The tassels tickle my cheeks, and my back arches in need. Claus runs the tassel between my asshole, dragging the leather fringes from my exit to my entrance, watching me drip onto the bed.

"My, my, my," he says. "Look at what I've done." He swings the flog one final time across my ass.

"Claus," I cry out.

"Yes, Cupid."

"I'm aching."

He kisses both of my cheeks. "Brace yourself."

He sticks his tongue inside my asshole, fucking it with a hungry appetite. I pull the sheets from the corner and stuff them in my mouth and take a breath when he pulls it out. His thumb circles my exit, and I revel in the filth, hunching his face while he travels around my private landing.

Back and forth I rock. Up and down he licks, massaging the inner linings of my jungle until I cum one final time. The whip lashes against me while I'm motionless and dazed with my ass in the air.

"Let me clean you up," he whispers, licking me dry everywhere I've trickled.

I look back at him, stroking his dick vigorously behind me. "That looks like fun." I smile at him.

"Wanna taste it?"

I nod out of curiosity, too late as I witness his jizz shoot out from the tip, and it warms my butt.

He smears and smoothes it on my skin. "Merry Christmas, Cupid."

I whisper, "Merry Christmas, Claus."

"Now go get cleaned up."

I inch back off the bed and stand before the stranger in my bedroom. We share a moment in the quiet between panting breaths and mutual admiration, then I make myself scarce and turn on the shower.

As it warms, I smile at myself in the mirror, eager to explore a deeper world of eroticism with the man I plan to marry.

I go back to the bedroom to thank Claus for the lesson and the release. And for keeping his word. But what I find is an empty room, scrambled sheets, and the card hanging on the edge of the bed.

CHAPTER 14

PENNY

The snowstorm has passed on, and the sun makes its first visible appearance in days. Before joining the ladies downstairs for breakfast, I pack my bags and realize my panties are missing.

I search for them under the bed and between the sheets. As I come up empty, I accept that Claus took them when he ghosted me.

I laugh out loud, then stop when I catch a glimpse of myself in the dresser mirror. Unsure if I feel shame, or grateful for what I've experienced in this room, I let out a long sigh, then take a moment to center myself before I join everyone downstairs.

As the snow melts and the town salts and clears the roads, we sit for one final breakfast.

Bellamy surprises all of us with gifts. "Don't open them until Christmas Day," she says.

After our final feast, we exchange information, take pictures, and say our goodbyes. Brent rolls the car around. His hands brush with Belise's when he hands her the keys.

"Where's the mistletoe when you need it?" he says.

Belise blushes. "Thank you for coming to our aid."

"It's been my pleasure."

Claire blows the horn and pulls out of the estate first.

I ask Belise, "What was that about?"

"I told y'all he had eyes for me."

She follows her lead to the main road for a few miles. The car is deathly silent. It feels like we're strangers stuck in an elevator shaft getting off on different floors.

"So we're not gonna talk about it?" Belise asks.

Cash points up ahead. "Claire wants you to pull over."

The signal on Claire's car blinks as she veers into a country general store lot. Belise pulls the car over, and we all hop out. Claire walks over, all smiles, bundled up in a raspberry wool coat and hat, and we stand on the side of the road, huddled like a football team.

"I spoke too soon at dinner last night." Claire checks out our surroundings. "Did you notice anything strange at the mansion?"

"Are you asking if we think Sam was telling the truth?"

"I was skirting around it, but yes." Her cheeks turn pink from the cold and embarrassment. "Once I sobered up, I had this eerie feeling like I was being watched in the house at all times." She points to Cash. "And I remember you were looking around when we were at breakfast that first morning. I assumed you felt it too."

Cash snickers. "That's one way to put it."

She and Belise look at each other.

"But yeah, I was looking for cameras that morning."

Claire's face flushes with relief. "Well, I swept my room and didn't find anything." She blows from her mouth. "But..."

"There's more?" I ask.

"Um...something else weird happened. I noticed a pair of panties that match one of my sets is missing."

Belise chokes on her spit. She and Cash glance at each other, then both of them look at me. I add nothing to the conversation.

"Same." Cash and Belise both admit.

Claire gasps. "So there was a thong thief roaming around from room to room." She claps her hands. "I bet it was Karl."

"I don't want to accuse anyone without any proof, ya know." Cash points to Belise. "And you asked if I thought it was the brother."

"He was so nice." Claire's voice lowers. "And hot."

The three of us give her a side-eye.

"Nothing happened there. I was just saying." She holds up her hands.

Belise asks her, "What do you think of Sam? And her story about Panty Claus now?"

Claire smacks her lips. "I think you just solved the mystery."

We look at her in confusion.

"Sam's the culprit. It had to be her snooping around to make us believe that cockamamie story she told us. Whew! I feel relieved. I mean, sorta. It is rather strange to steal panties from women to prove your point. Am I right?"

"You are," Cash butts in.

"Well, thank you ladies for stopping. The missing panty debacle would have had me puzzled for I don't know how long."

I chime in. "Well, we better get going. What's left of our holiday is waiting for us. You be safe."

"You ladies do the same."

We get back in the car and sit there for a while. The radio is off. And the bypassing traffic shakes the car like a rocking chair.

"Noowww, are we gonna talk about it?"

Everyone looks their own way. The car remains quiet, and the experiences at the house are becoming more and more real and not a figment of the imagination.

"We never leave a place and have nothing to say." Belise points out. "I fucked Panty Claus."

"You did!" Cash rubs her shoulder. "Good for you! I told you we could have had a threesome."

"Say what?" I ask.

Cash smiles at me. "Oh, I fucked him too. Twice."

"Twice!" Belise and I say at the same time.

"You have no idea how hard it was to not rub that in Sam's face."

"Damn." Belise shakes her head. "He sure has a lot of free time on his hands."

Cash raises a brow. "And stamina." She turns to me. "Anything you wanna share, Pen?"

I laugh at them. "Nice try. Cash, you said yourself, you embellish sometimes to liven up a crowd. I don't believe this made-up story. For all I know, you planned for Claire to pull us over and feed this tall tale you have been trying to sell me all weekend."

Belise cranks the car and merges into traffic. She drives for at least a mile then grills me.

"So, everyone had an experience, but you?"

"It's cool if it did. We won't judge you." Cash does her best to pull a confession from me.

I look out at rows of melting trees with icicles dangling like frozen spears and keep my face hidden so they can't see the indulgent guilt that'll forever be my secret. With a sly grin, I end the inquisition and say, "Nope. Guess I wasn't his type."

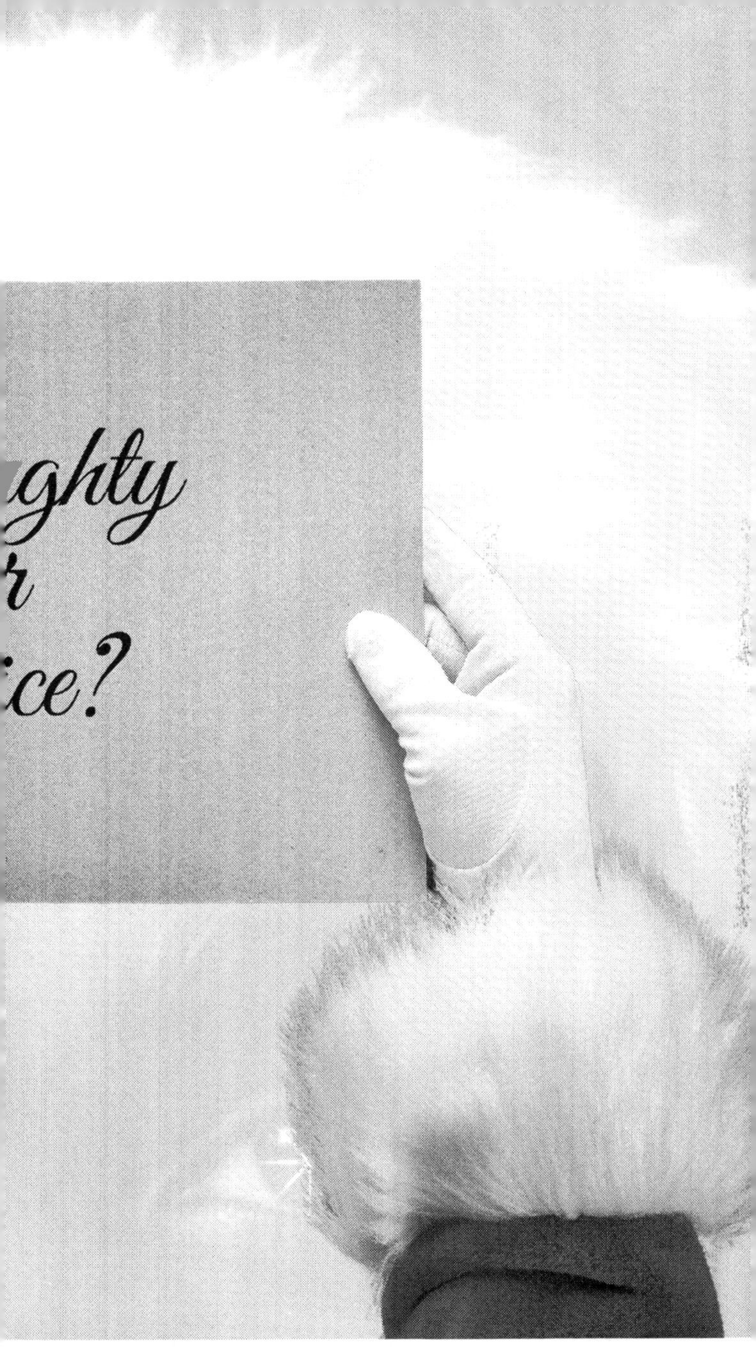
ghty
r
ce?

RIDDLE ME THIS

DEAR NAUGHTY READER

- Is Panty Claus real?
- If your answer is yes, then who do you think it is?
- If your answer is no, then what do you think he is? A ghost? A shifter? A spirit? Or...?
- Would you have slept with Panty Claus?
- Why hasn't Panty Claus ever visited Bellamy?
- Did you notice the significance of the animals mentioned?
- Have you ever heard of parallel cities?

Find me on Facebook, Instagram, or Bluesky and let's begin a thread with your answers. I can't wait to see your responses. 😄

For an alternate ending, subscribe to my newsletter:

https://dl.bookfunnel.com/nc50v9t8o8

Fine with the ending you've read,
stay in touch with me here instead.

thembp.kit.com

Thank You

Thank you in advance to everyone that will leave a review of my first Christmas novella on all the platforms, and spread the word about it as word of mouth is the best gift an author can receive. Especially around the holidays. I hope you had a jolly good time reading Panty Claus.

 MBP

About the Author

Mahogany B. Preston is a North Charleston, S.C. native who loves plants, being outdoors, and learning new trades. She considers herself to be a professional student as she satisfies her curiosity by enrolling in free courses, no matter the subject.

As an emerging author whose body of work features romantic comedies, humorous holiday women's fiction, and witty novellas. Her specialty is banter, making her audience enjoy a chuckle or two.

Mahogany hopes that one day her love of knowledge will reveal the true secret of life. If she uncovers that mystery, she will then have to decide if she should share it.

Please sign up for her newsletter and follow her on the featured social media platforms to stay in touch.

thembp.kit.com

Manufactured by Amazon.ca
Bolton, ON

43643916R00068